The Book You Need Before You Buy That Accounting Software

How Find, Buy and Implement the Best Accounting Software Solution for Your Business

By

Jeff Lewis

BY JEFF LEWIS

www.jefflewis.com.au

jeff@usagebusiness.com

All rights reserved. No part of this book may be reproduced or transmitted in any form or by any means, electronic or mechanical, including photocopying, recording or by any information storage and retrieval system, without written permission from the authors, except for the inclusion of brief quotations in a review.

Limit of Liability Disclaimer: The information contained in this book is for information purposes only, and may not apply to your situation. The author, publisher, distributor and provider provide no warranty about the content or accuracy of content enclosed. Information provided is subjective. Keep this in mind when reviewing this guide.

Neither the Publisher nor Authors shall be liable for any loss of profit or any other commercial damages resulting from use of this guide. All links are for information purposes only and are not warranted for content, accuracy, or any other implied or explicit purpose.

Earnings Disclaimer: All income examples in this book are just that – examples. They are not intended to represent or guarantee that everyone will achieve the same results. You understand that each individual's success will be determined by his or her desire, dedication, background, effort and motivation to work. There is no guarantee you will duplicate any of the results stated here. You recognize any business endeavor has inherent risk of loss of capital.

"The typical result one can expect to achieve is nothing. The "typical" person never gets to the end of this book. The "typical" person fails to implement anything. Thus they earn nothing. Zero. No income. And perhaps a loss of income. That's because "typical" people do nothing and therefore they achieve nothing. Be atypical. Do something. Implement something. If it doesn't work; make a change…and implement that. Try again…try harder. Persist. And reap the rewards."

Copyright © 2015 by Jeff Lewis

ISBN-13:978-1505420425

FOREWORD

Running a small, medium or large size business today has never been more demanding. The complexities involved in record keeping, accounting, tax, and other management tasks take up significant resources and time. And with profits always in mind, finding ways to stay competitive and building a robust set of systems, it can seem all too hard to invest the time required to optimise those accounting and management software solutions.

Before I started to read through Jeff Lewis' book on how to choose an accounting software package, I did wonder if this was going to be another self-promotion marketing e-book. What a pleasant surprise this book turned out to be.

The probing and comprehensive issues Jeff raises for any business on how to choose accounting and business management software are not only welcome, but from a truly objective and experienced perspective. The Internet is now an overwhelming and not particularly trustworthy destination when it comes to finding rigorous, unbiased and dependable advice on matters of commercial importance.

Jeff asks the right questions and gives the kind of insightful tips his experience affords. Having previously held the position of Director of Sage Pastel International for nine years, Jeff was responsible for establishing the international platform for distributing Sage Pastel products globally to 52 countries.

I thoroughly recommend this book to all business owners, directors and accounting managers looking to tap into the sort of knowledge you just can't get by Googling or relying on the reseller or rep from of an accounting software supplier.   **Dr Harvey May , December, 2014**

Contents

About the author 1

Introduction 4

Chapter 1: Why is Accounting Software important? 7

Business management systems and Business Excellence 8
What can (ERP) accounting software do for you? 9

Why picking the right ERP system matters 11

Chapter 2: Create a plan for successful software selection 12

Learn about the software systems available 13
Define your objects for software implementation 13
Justify the software in terms of financial gains 13
It's not just the new software: People matter more 14
Analyze your Business needs and resources in detail 15
Find the best product for your business 16
Plan ahead 17
Identify the stakeholders 17
How does the reseller fit with your plans? 18
Installing and implementing the solution 18
Managing the software after implementation 19
Assess your strengths and weaknesses 19
Other areas for analysis 20

Chapter 3: Getting organized in your search 23

Basic initial research 23

Functional factors you should look out for: 24

Basic requirements accounting software should have: 26

    Integration with other systems is critical 29

Determine project success factors 33

The critical elements that contribute to the success or failure. 33

Considering the software implementation risks 36

Chapter 4: Comparing prices 38

Total cost of ownership 38

Common fees and expenses for "On-Premises" systems 39

Common fees and expenses for (SaaS) 41

Comparing the quotes 43

Chapter 5: Assess the software vendor's viability 44

What about the reseller or Business Partner? 46

Chapter 6: Implementing the New Accounting Software 49

The best implementation strategy 49

Tips for successful accounting software implementation 51

Software implementation game plan checklist 53

Going beyond the Accounting Software Implementation 54

Reporting, dashboards and alerts 54

Training employees 54

Training for new employees 55

Regular system analysis 56

The annual business check-up 56

Chapter 7: Summary 58

Chapter 8: Next Steps 59

Chapter 9: Case studies 63

GET YOUR BOOK BONUS TODAY:

To get access to our special 55 Page "Software Selection and Implementation Checklist"

Visit www.jefflewis.com.au and email us your receipt as per instructions on the website.

Or Scan this QR Code:

About the author

Jeff Lewis from **Usage Business Solutions** has been a part of **Sage Accounting Solutions** since June 2000. Jeff was born in Cleveland, Ohio, USA and attended Ohio State University. Jeff began his sales and sales management career in the Midwest as a sales professional with US Steel. Sales management experience and a Sales Management Apprenticeship Programme with Zig Ziglar opened the door to vast opportunities on the East Coast of the USA.

With a strong desire to be number one in his field, Jeff moved to Washington D.C. with AGIP Oil. This led to opportunities for living and working abroad, namely in Puerto Rico, Venezuela, France, Israel and Egypt, where he developed country specific initiatives and built distribution centers. Utilizing local talent and combining it with proven management methods, he achieved the establishment of successful centers operating to this day throughout these territories. International business development became Jeff's primary focus. Whilst in South Africa on holidays Jeff discovered opportunities within the freight and logistics arena and began working with AEI, BAX Global and then Fritz Companies (UPS) as Sales Director for Africa. His primary focus was to identify opportunities within Africa including joint ventures, acquisitions, agency options, branch operations and franchise style options and he soon became an expert in this field.

From there Jeff migrated into the I.T. field with Ariel Technologies, developing the Sun Microsystems platform within the group in Africa.

When the opportunity arose to join Ariel Technologies, Jeff migrated to information technology within the Sun Micro environment, developing skills related to governmental infrastructure and foundational based high end scale solutions for larger corporate customers.

In July 2000, Jeff embarked on a mission to establish **Sage Pastel Software** internationally.

Sage Software is listed on the London Stock Exchange and now has over 6 million users globally with 12,700 employees in 24 countries.

Jeff's business development methodology positioned Sage Pastel to become a serious market player in numerous foreign markets. Starting from a zero base, Jeff has built the division to the current position:

- ❖ 85 Business Partner distribution agents
- ❖ 52 countries
- ❖ 450 resellers

The Book You Need Before You Buy That Accounting Software   *www.jefflewis.com.au*

- 180,000 companies utilizing our software applications
- 340,000 end users operating our applications daily
- 13,500 + students certified on our programs
- 50+ Authorized training centers internationally

In 2009 Jeff immigrated to Australia and established **Usage Business Solutions**, the Channel Partner for the region. Since Usage Business Solutions' establishment Jeff has continued to build a network of resellers and distributors in over 55 countries, and has won numerous Sage sales awards.

Usage Business prides itself on customer care and expertise with more than 75 years of combined experience in software products.

Usage Business Solutions in Australia and New Zealand has a network of 40 qualified Business Partners who provide quality on-site implementation and consulting services. Their focus is the small to medium sized business market and specialises in easy to use and powerful accounting and ERP solutions.

For more information visit www.usagebusiness.com

Introduction

Fundamentally a business management system should be the core of any company, second only to its staff. In some respects you might think of the business management system as the organization's communications system; receiving data from one point or another, manipulating that data, and then allowing it to be shared among those people and groups who need it. As a direct result of this critical position, business management systems represent either an opportunity for improved business success or the beginning of a slide toward mediocrity or even failure.

In our experience most business owners or managers are simply not aware that there are better solutions in the marketplace. The hidden losses in any business occur when staff are performing tasks that are labor intensive involving hours of manual work in order to produce a result. Often these procedures can be streamlined or enhanced with the right solution and could repay the investment with just one area improved in your business!

The challenge for most business owners or managers is that they are simply too busy to stop to plan and research superior systems, sometimes relying on their internal personnel to advise them, or just avoiding change and the perceived upheaval and cost involved to even begin the process.

Overall, the marketplace is littered with companies who could be performing more efficiently and profitably than they are right now.

The Number One desire we are nearly always asked for is

- ❖ Better reporting
- ❖ Accurate information available quickly

The business management system can do nothing by itself, absolutely nothing. Success requires dedicated people working together toward a set of common objectives.

Your business management system is but one of the elements that contribute to this potential for success. Yes, the potential is there, but everything else has to be present in order for the business management system to achieve its potential.

This book is designed to help you manage your way through

the minefield of choices and industry hype and find the best solution for your company.

So let's get to it and start your search for the best accounting product for your business!

Chapter 1: Why is Accounting Software important?

When you start your own business, your main goal will be creating profits for your company. In order to achieve this, it is important that you analyze all your risks carefully since no profit comes without some risk. Care must be taken in managing risks, or your company will more than likely fail, instead of making a profit. One of the challenges that you'll have to face once you set up your business is ensuring that all the finances of your business are managed properly on daily basis. This factor is a clear identifier in choosing the right business software product for you.

Some key factors that you need to consider:

- In our experience it's failing to ask the right questions that can result in a wrong buying decision.
- Most business owners only buy accounting software every 5-7 years and lack the time to research the thousands of products on the market.

If on the other hand, you are a growing organization, at some point in your business expansion, you will start experiencing frustration with the limitations of entry-level accounting software or start-up software for the small enterprise. Entry level software is not designed to be multi-faceted nor multi-functional. Nor is it designed to be business management focused. That usually means more reliance on pesky manual processes, annoying spreadsheets, extra time and extra effort - not to mention double-entry and re-keying data into software not capable of accommodating your growing requirements.

This is where mid-tier ERP and Business Management Solutions are targeted at, software designed to incorporate aspects of the entire business operation. Software built to manage multiple companies and even multi aspects of layers of the business. Priced to compete in this growth space of the market, yet easy to use, scalable solutions suit smaller businesses that are also growing up.

Business management systems and Business Excellence

Business management systems will achieve nothing if the people, processes and culture that surround them offer no assistance or do not contribute to the same business objectives. Your main task is the creation of a foundation that will help you move to a more profitable future, not duplicate your past. However, it is but one element among several that must be analysed, improved and monitored on a continuous basis.

This book has been devoted to improving your business through Business Excellence and finding the right solution for you; let us move forward by leaving you with the definition of Business Excellence that will serve as our foundation as we build this better future starting tomorrow.

"Business Excellence is dedicated people working with and serving other equally dedicated people so that both can achieve shared and mutually beneficial goals."

What can (ERP) accounting software do for you?

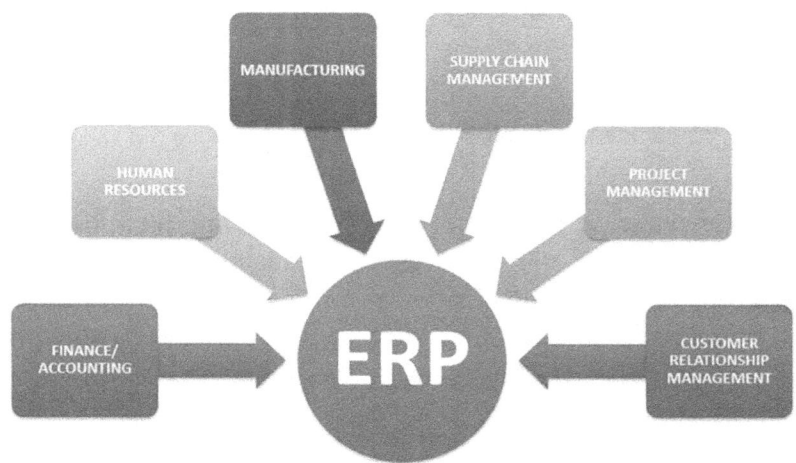

As a small or even mid-sized business manager, it is often difficult for you to have a proper accountant on your payroll to handle your finances, this is why you need Enterprise Resource Planning (ERP). Most owners and managers are time poor, juggling many facets of the business whilst struggling to keep up with accounting procedures.

An ERP accounting software system is used for effectively keeping track of the finances of your business on a daily basis. An ERP will help manage things like, cash flow recording, business report generation, account receivables and account payables schedules. It's easy to believe you're managing as it is, but questions need to be asked;

- ❖ Could your time be spent more wisely?

- ❖ Do you routinely have enough time for tax planning throughout the year?
- ❖ Is our business the best it can be?
- ❖ Is tax time a breeze?

If you answered "No" to any of these, there's a good chance your current system is letting you down.

With time, your accounting data builds into an indispensable repository of data. Performance based software gives you reporting at your fingertips, catering for legislation and taxation changes. More importantly it provides you with the assurance of your data being safe. Imagine losing it!

Accounting software products like **Sage Evolution** also adhere to and apply global financial requirements as set out by the IFRS (International Financial Reporting Standards). These are principles-based standards, interpretations and the framework (1989) adopted by the International Accounting Standards Board (IASB). By using an IFRS certified product, you can be sure your business is meeting its reporting obligations – worldwide!

ERP accounting software will also streamline all your accounting functions over a single platform, organizing your financial data and making it easier for you to make the necessary business calculations. Features include automating accounting functions, such as payroll management, tax management, tracking salaries and bonuses, while preparing other financial data that can eliminate the need for making spreadsheets. If you're striving for the best for your company, implementation of an ERP accounting software is what you need to consider in achieving this aim.

Why picking the right ERP system matters

There isn't any doubt about the fact that an ERP accounting software system can make your business highly efficient, bringing accuracy to all your financial calculations. However, your choice of software requires careful consideration. Researching the market will give you a plethora of options, offering different features and benefits. It can be a daunting task to know what's right for you, random selection is dangerous as you may end up with an inappropriate system resulting in added expenses to make it work for you. This leads to a frustrating, expensive and time consuming outcome.

Therefore, before you choose the accounting software for your company, you first have to understand what your company needs. Software that is designed for small to medium businesses is completely different from software that is marketed to large organizations, offering different features to match their needs. If you have just started your business, you will probably be working alone and getting a system that caters to and offers access to 100 people won't be of any use. Considering the fact that the software cost is based on your usage, it is essential to analyze the minimum software requirements of your business first before you select anything.

We are going to teach you how to pick up the right accounting software for your business. Sound good?

For those who are currently facing this decision, this book acts as a comprehensive guide so you can achieve the best, most cost-effective and highly functional ERP accounting software for your organization.

Chapter 2: Create a plan for successful software selection

Selecting Enterprise Resource Planning software for your business isn't always the easiest decision to make. There are a lot of things that need to be done before deciding on the right software from the market for your business. From gathering detailed information to proper implementation and management, every step is going to be a challenge in itself when you decide to employ a new software system for your organization. The more employees your business has, the more difficult it will be to manage the changes in systems and make the right decisions about which would be the right system for you.

For all that, what you need first is a plan that outlines what your objectives and strategies are, and how you expect the software to perform. Depending on how big or small your organization is you can tailor this plan to your business accordingly as it covers all the necessary steps but some of them might not be needed for your business. Write a list, right now, start with the basics and expand it until it becomes your wish list. Then prioritize the points, this will be a great starting point.

Learn about the software systems available

Before you start, the most important thing to do is to educate yourself about what your options are when it comes to software selection. There are different types of business software solutions that are available in the market like accounting software, ERP software and CRM software, all serving a different objective. You need to understand how each software package is different from the others, and whether or not it can help you achieve the target you are aiming for. If the benefits you are striving to achieve aren't there in the software you are planning to get, your entire project might fail without yielding any positive results.

Define your objects for software implementation

Before you start worrying about software choices, you first need to define your objectives in detail so that you know exactly what you want to achieve from this software implementation. These objectives can be simple or complex, measured or subjective, but the point is that they should be there to provide you with a performance measurement benchmark in the end to show you whether your software implementation project turned out successful or not.

Justify the software in terms of financial gains

Just because a program can help you meet your objectives doesn't make it the right choice; you need to consider whether it's worth the price you pay for it or not. There is no use getting software that is going to cost you more that it can benefit you. Whether you invest $300 or $30,000 in the new software, you need to justify this investment cost by calculating how much profit it can eventually bring to your company. Many business managers make the mistake of getting software just to automate their operations, assuming it will always be beneficial, and end up incurring more costs and inefficiencies than before.

It's not just the new software: People matter more

When it comes to successfully achieving the objectives you were expecting to get from the software, there is one major aspect you need to consider and manage carefully – your people. That won't be much of a problem if you are a small business manager but the more employees you have, the more difficult it will be to manage change in the system. The easiest way to deal with this issue is to keep your employees involved all the way, right from the start. Just like you, your employees need to be educated about what the software can do and why it is important for the company and encourage them to embrace this change.

The key is to make them feel involved in the entire procedure so that they can be more comfortable with the final purchase decision. As the users of the software, they reserve the right to criticize the system beforehand if they find it lacking or inappropriate in any way. You can hold educational sessions to tell your employees more about the software, concluding it with brainstorming sessions where they could openly give their own suggestions regarding the software and its benefits for the company.

Analyze your Business needs and resources in detail

Next, you need to find out what are the specific needs of your business that you are seeking to have fulfilled from the software you are planning to implement. Do you need more efficiency in your business operations? Do you want the operations to be more streamlined and integrated with each other? Find out the key operational areas where your business isn't the most productive and think how the software you'll select will bring efficiency to those areas.

After that, you need to analyze your own resources, structures, and procedures to determine which type of software would be best suited to you. Are your employees skilled enough to use the software efficiently? Do you have the necessary hardware required to run the system? Do you already have streamlined processes that would be disturbed if the new software was installed? Take a closer look at how the implementation of this new software would impact the current operations and resources management of your organization.

Find the best product for your business

Now that you know everything about what the ideal software for your business should have in it, you can start negotiating with the vendors to get the best possible software solution. It's important that you consider your vendors as your business partners if you want to come up with a more tailored and customized solution. Look at a few different products your vendor is offering to you, and discuss the possible changes that can be made to these products so that they better suit your specific requirements. A lot of vendors will easily agree to make major changes to the basic software to make it just the way you want, albeit at a slightly higher cost.

Plan ahead

Begin planning to upgrade before you are forced to do so and make the change while your business is running smoothly. Define your goals and objectives and try to anticipate how your business is likely to grow over a period of at least five to ten years - will the system you are purchasing be suitable for this period?

Some questions to consider asking yourself:

- ✓ What changes are the business likely to expect as it grows?
- ✓ What are the key challenges that the business is likely to encounter?
- ✓ Will your customer base change?
- ✓ Will you be selling to a larger customer base?
- ✓ Will you be adding new stores/locations?
- ✓ Will you sell to an international market?
- ✓ Will you sell products or services via the Internet?
- ✓ Will your business purchases include international goods or services?

Identify the stakeholders

It is important to identify and include all the stakeholders at the beginning of the decision making process as the decision to implement new software is likely to impact a wide variety of people and departments throughout the company.

User friendly and intuitive navigating is often a request, but employees may need to have access to customer data with real-time information and where the accounting software readily integrates with your existing applications. Software applications must be capable of importing and retrieving information from other areas of your business allowing CFO's the flexibility to produce and customise various reports.

How does the reseller fit with your plans?

The path you have chosen assumes that the product recommended by the reseller with whom you are currently working will meet your requirements. You need to feel comfortable with the reseller and the product's ability to meet your most critical requirements.

Installing and implementing the solution

After you have decided which software solution is best for your business, the next step is its careful implementation. While it might seem like the most important thing, it's actually the easiest to manage compared to all that comes before and after it. Implementation is just a series of physical tasks that can be managed well if you get the right professionals to do it. However, there are certain complications that can occur when it comes to implementation, mainly time restrictions and operations management.

It is important that, while the system is being implemented and integrated with your business functions, the daily operations of your business aren't disturbed because of it. You should ensure that the implementation is completed within a preset time frame and doesn't cause too much lag or inconvenience in your daily business operations that can lead to too many losses.

Managing the software after implementation

Once the system is implemented, your work isn't finished; it's time to monitor the success. Now is the time to look back at those objectives you made initially and see if they are being fulfilled according to the plan now that the software is implemented. There are several things that might not go according to the plan you had in mind; one of the main problems is that of people having trouble adjusting to the new changes. All these post-implementation issues need to be addressed and resolved to ensure that the software is being used in the most efficient manner, and then it should be observed whether the objectives are being met or not.

Assess your strengths and weaknesses

One vital first task would be to identify those processes that have a direct effect on the business management system or are affected directly by it. In some cases you may have to wait until you actually select the system to complete this analysis, for some business management systems affect business processes in different ways.

Once you have determined the depth of the improvement analysis, you can break these tasks into specific areas. This analysis of strengths and weaknesses needs to be split into those factors that affect the business management system and those that do not and are therefore candidates for business improvement initiatives, either now or later.

Although you may have elected not to initiate any business improvement tasks until after the new accounting system has been installed, don't rule out scheduling one or more now.

Remember that an analysis doesn't necessarily mean something is wrong.

Other areas for analysis

Strategic Management

What information does management need to measure the success of existing ventures, analyse projected revenues and costs of new ventures, track in detail the revenues and costs of new ventures of the company?

Sales and Marketing

How well do you track and control the prospecting cycle? Do you lose more new business opportunities than you should? What should you be doing differently? How can technology or software help you improve the effectiveness and efficiency of your sales and marketing efforts?

Customer Service

How well do you believe you manage your customers? How well do your customers believe you manage them? What improvements can you make or should you make in order to serve your customers more effectively? What is the cost of such initiatives? How can software and technology help you serve your customers better?

Production Management

How well do you manage the order-to-delivery process? How well do you integrate your customers into this cycle? Can you shorten the order-to-delivery cycle? What do your customers want? How can technology and software help you manage the production cycle better?

Production Efficiency

How does your cost of production compare with your own projections and those of similar companies or industries? What can you do to reduce your production costs without affecting customer service, delivery times or quality? How can technology and software help you reduce production costs?

Personnel Efficiency

How skilled are your employees compared to the demands of their jobs? What specific training, internal support, incentives or job restructuring is required to give employees the tools, skills and motivation to work more effectively and efficiently? How can software assist you in these efforts?

Financial Management

Are you tracking the right combination of revenues and costs? Are you confident that the allocations of costs, particularly overhead costs, are an accurate representation of the activities necessary to create, produce, sell and support specific products or product groups? Do you understand all of the factors that contribute to your financial success (or failure)? Do you produce reports at the right time and with the right level of detail to support the decision making process? How can software help you manage your financial affairs more effectively?

Chapter 3: Getting organized in your search

It's not always easy to pick out the best ERP accounting software for your company from the huge array that is available in the market. Making the right decision requires you to spend a lot of time and effort on the whole software evaluation process before you can make an actual purchase decision. Here is a systematic step-by-step guide that will tell you how you should go about picking the best software for your company.

Basic initial research

Before you launch into your analysis, you might want to spend some time on research or background knowledge accumulation. The more you know about software selection, the industry in which you compete, and specific functions that may be of interest to you, the better prepared you and others will be when you begin your analysis. The following list of information resources might assist.

- Internet Search
- Industry journals
- Computer magazines
- Ask your accountant
- Friends
- Competitors
- Trade shows
- Seminars
- Chamber of Commerce
- Consultants

Functional factors you should look out for:

Functionality is the first thing you need to focus on when it comes to making a selection, and for that you need to consider the functional factors most carefully. Here are some of these factors explained:

> **The Data Collection System –** In order to determine whether the software is able to provide you with the reports you need or not, it is important to assess how it collects data from different sources and streamline the most vital parts of it to make decisions. Knowing in which particular critical areas your selected software will work well is extremely important to understand what outcome you can expect from it.

> **Reporting Capabilities of the Software –** Having all your data at a single source isn't all that you need from good accounting software. You also need properly generated reports that you can interpret and use for decision making, and that is what

comprehensive software should provide. You should see that the software you have selected not only offers extensive reporting capabilities but also extracts them instantly when needed in critical situations.

- **Upgrades and Updates for the Software** – Another important thing to ensure is that your software vendor is willing to offer you a flexible and scalable system, and a well-developed maintenance program. For accounting software to be the best, it needs to be maintained, updated and upgraded regularly so that bugs can be fixed and new specifications can be added. While such vendors might charge you a bit extra, it can be well worth it because no maintenance can be a risk for your data safety and security.

- **Ease of Use** – The best accounting software is always one that is easy to use, even for individuals who are not too good at handling accounts. It should be simple enough in its functionality, interface and navigation that you or anyone else who is supposed to use it can do so without much difficulty or needing proper extensive training beforehand.

- **Access Allowed to Users** – Depending on the size of your company, you will have to decide how many users will require access to the system. If you have a small business, there is no use paying extra charges for user accessibility for a lot of people. Similarly, for large businesses, software that allows only single-person access is useless.

> **Data Validation Structure** – For an accounting software to be effective, it should be efficient in catching errors in data and making necessary attempts for validation. If the vendor information is duplicated, the items are labeled incorrectly or the amounts entered seem unusually high, the software must identify and alarm you to such an incident right away.

Basic requirements accounting software should have:

The requirements you should look out for in an accounting software depend on what your business needs are, which would vary from buyer to buyer. However, there are some minimum requirements that all good and reliable accounting software should have, which include the capability to:

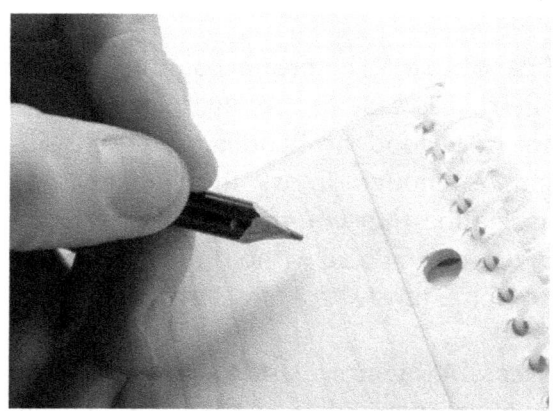

- ✓ Improve functions like asset management, inventory, and order placement and tracking.

- ✓ Give multiple users access to the financial data so they can work with it.

- ✓ Store supplier and customer data in an organized manner.

- ✓ Track sales and create business statement and sales invoices for the customers.

- ✓ Enable forecast methodologies and refine them continuously to improve efficiency of operations and effective pricing insights.

- ✓ Create different reports such as tax reports, budget reports and other annual and monthly reports.

- ✓ Track purchase orders to record the correct amount of inventory.

In addition to these basic requirements, you can look for features that further suit your business software needs. Your final selection criteria for the software should be based on all these functional features along with other factors like the total cost of the software, its reporting capabilities, the ease of use it offers, interoperability and scalability limits, and the support services offered by the vendors.

The chosen software solution you select will depend on the type of business you are operating, whether you are a sole-proprietorship, a medium sized business or a corporate entity.

Minimum requirements to expect from your software:

- ✓ Multiple users to work with financial data
- ✓ Integrate easily with existing software
- ✓ Enable and refine forecasting methodologies for improved production efficiency and deliver more effective pricing inputs
- ✓ Improve order, inventory, and asset management
- ✓ Store customer and supplier data
- ✓ Create invoices & statements
- ✓ Track sales
- ✓ Track of inventory through purchase order
- ✓ Create budget report
- ✓ Create monthly and annual reports
- ✓ Business tax reporting

The software application must address all your business and specific industry requirements or have additional 3rd party add-ons that can fill that gap. Most established vendors have Software Development Kits (SDK modules) that allow independent software solution partners/developers to create products that work with the core business management application.

Identifying the unique attributes of your company will assist in differentiating the necessary features from the nice to have features. It is also important to understand what the software can do and what its limitations are.

If you use tools from the Microsoft Office Suite, make sure that the system you choose can fully leverage this software. Think about the following:

- ✓ Is it easy to create business reports and manage data using Excel?

- ✓ Will your solution synchronize with Outlook so that you can seamlessly create quotes; enter orders, track sales and initiate marketing campaigns while working from within the Outlook program?

These are the types of issues you will want to explore to ensure that you get the system that is right for your company.

Integration with other systems is critical

One of the most important factors you should take into account when introducing new accounting software in your company is how well it will integrate with the existing systems. In order to improve the efficiency of your business operations, which is the main goal behind any software implementation, it is important that you have a complete view of real-time information regarding your business.

This complete view requires that all major and minor systems and applications used in your organization are completely integrated, offering you a flawless data transition flow. For that reason, good accounting software should always have the capability of retrieving and importing data from other business areas without any flaw or delay. This means it should always offer industry standards that integrate well with other systems used in your organization.

There is any number of tools, features and functions that might help you improve certain business processes or help individual people carry out their job responsibilities more efficiently or effectively.

Functional possibilities

- ✓ **Contact management:** Contact management can become a valuable sales and marketing tool, particularly for companies whose sales cycle tends to be quite lengthy or complex, or where there are a large number of customers who require some form of management.
- ✓ **Credit management:** Credit management is very effective if you extend facilities for your customers. This establishes a credit application system for new customers, as well as a credit watch system for existing customers.
- ✓ **Collections management:** A collections management module can and should be used by all organizations. It's very easy to let a customer drag their payments out, or not pay until they are faced with legal action.
- ✓ **Procurement:** In larger businesses having a workflow for purchasing can be an efficient and cost saving process.
- ✓ **Cash management:** Proper management of your cash flow is vital for every business.

- ✓ **Exception management:** Few products support these functions in depth but having system alerts and ability to track exceptions can be a vital process in a busy business.

Reporting possibilities

- ✓ **Built-in report writers:** Rather than having to rely on a third party report writer, look first to the system itself. If your reporting requirements are not that complex, the system's report writer might be robust enough.
- ✓ **Support for leading third party report writers:** While all products support some form of internal report writer, most don't come close to the functionality of third party report writers.
- ✓ **Internal graphing capabilities:** Graphs are a visual representation of numerical information. Many people find it easier to interpret information visually, rather than reading though a report.
- ✓ **Metrics and dashboards:** Many vendors are beginning to understand the inherent value of Executive Information Systems and graphical presentations of critical information.
- ✓ **Report scheduling:** Many detailed reports, even long financial reports, don't need to be viewed the minute they are printed. Rather than tying up valuable printer time during a busy day, these reports can be scheduled to print automatically at night or at some other more convenient time.
- ✓ **Drilldown analysis:** If a Balance Sheet or Income Statement line item seems to be excessive, drilldown analysis allows users to see the transactions behind

the summary totals. This can be a valuable audit and analysis tool.
- ✓ **Hot links to spreadsheets and word processors:** One of the best examples of the value of establishing a hot link between a business management system and a spreadsheet is budgeting. Few, if any, business management systems support anything other than very simple budget preparation.

Technological possibilities

- ✓ **Workflow management**: All companies create specific methodologies by which certain processes are managed. Purchasing and credit approval are ideal examples. Technology has allowed these processes to be automated where one person completes their specific task, and the electronic information is passed on to the next person in the chain automatically. This reduces time delays while the information is being passed from one person to another, and increases control at the same time because the system itself tracks where the information is at any point in time.

- ✓ **Document management**: Document management is an extension of workflow management. Here an electronic picture of the source document can accompany the information itself. In addition, document management eliminates the necessity of storing the paper document, or allows users to store paper documents in a more logical fashion.
- ✓ **E-commerce:** While electronic commerce does offer the possibility of selling goods over the Internet 24 hours per day with no human intervention (therefore

reducing the processing costs to zero), electronic commerce isn't a guaranteed profit source. You have to be in the right business selling the right products to the right customer base. Creating and maintaining web pages isn't cheap, particularly for larger organizations. The more diverse or customer driven your pricing tends to be, the more difficult web page design and maintenance becomes.
- ✓ **Knowledge management**: The data within a business management system is but one source of knowledge. The experience and personal knowledge of each employee is more valuable than any of the information in the business management system. The only problem is how to share this information with a large number of people.

Determine project success factors

The critical elements that contribute to the success or failure.

- ✓ **The owner/manager must support the process:** Once the decision has been made to automate, the project must be allowed to proceed to its natural completion. The only method of ensuring this is for the owner of the business (or department manager) to give his or her blessing, and active support. This is one of the most critical success factors.

- ✓ **The owner/manager must be willing to change:** This is not the same thing. While support for automation might ensure that the project is completed, the inability or unwillingness to change the way a company operates will block or stop any positive impact that automation may create. The owner/manager must accept the fact that automation may require changes throughout the company, not just in the accounting department. The fact that the owner/manager does not trust the figures produced or refuses to modify certain business strategies will dampen everyone's enthusiasm for the project, if not completely kill it.

- ✓ **Everyone must be involved in the process:** Remember that new technology may be disconcerting to some people, and that new processes cannot be imposed on people without there being some resistance. The project will not end with the installation of the chosen product. Those people who will use the system must be involved in the decision making process right from the start. If a system is imposed on them, there is a greater risk that they will consciously or unconsciously fight the system once installed. Their active participation in the process might even bring to light opportunities or issues that might be missed otherwise.
- ✓ **Just one Project Leader!** While the involvement of each person is vitally important, this doesn't mean the project should be managed by a committee. The appointment of one person as coordinator will ensure that the project doesn't go off track. Committees are effective at oversight and making the final purchase decision, but committees are lousy when it comes to management of projects on a daily basis.
- ✓ **The project manager must have everyone's support**: The project manager must be given the authority to direct everyone's activities. At the same time the

project manager must realize that there is a significant difference between leading a project and becoming a general. Both factors must be present. Decisions must be made, and tasks assigned. The project manager (with the active support of the owner/ manager) must have the authority to delegate responsibility and make events happen. The efficiency with which these tasks are carried out will be greater if people respect the decisions of the project manager. Does this sound simple? It really might be one of the most difficult tasks in the whole automation process.

- ✓ **The existing manual business management system must be efficient:** Analysing and improving the manual side of the business management system should be your first task. Implementing automation will not fix an inefficient or ineffective information processing system. Automated business management systems will not achieve their ideal potential if the underlying methods by which information is processed are inefficient.

Please don't forget these points:

- ✓ **The company itself must be well organized:** The methods by which you choose to operate your business are more critical than any one business management system. You must understand what your company must do well to succeed, organize it to achieve that goal, and provide your employees with an environment in which they can achieve success on a personal level. Your employees must be given the tools, the environment, and the motivation to succeed. Without these factors being available, the business management system itself stands little chance of having any impact.

- ✓ **A realistic budget must be prepared**: A new automated business management is an asset whose purchase must be justified by some financial return. You must determine very accurately what the total cost of this investment will be. The cost of the hardware and software is but one part of the total investment in automation. The budget you establish must be realistic.

Considering the software implementation risks

Implementation of new software is accompanied by risk but if you choose software that is inadequate, this risk can go up substantially. The major risk that inadequate accounting software can pose for your business is the inability to detect theft or fraud automatically. However, there are other risks to consider as well which include:

- ➢ **Incorrect information entry or loss of data during or after implementation:** If the data is entered incorrectly during the manual data entry process, or is completely ignored due to human error, this can lead to completely inaccurate business reports.

- ➢ **No backup of the accounting software in case of loss of service:** If your business is completely reliant on the software, this can disrupt your business operations and cause data and financial losses

- **No adequate return on your investment:** For most business managers, getting new software means saving time and making their business more efficient. However, the investment isn't always justified due to the recurring costs. Maintenance and staff training costs are two major areas of concerns here, especially in industries where staff turnover rate is extremely high.

- **Vulnerability to viruses resulting in loss of data:** Computer software systems are always vulnerable to different kinds of viruses, Trojans and malicious sabotage attempts that, when successful, can lead to breach of confidential customer data and privacy, or loss of crucial business data.

- **The ever-present threat of hacking:** When it comes to online transactions and systems, there is always a risk of the systems getting hacked, compromising crucial data like credit card information. While most software systems use SSL encryptions for protection, there might still be weak points in the coding that offer hackers a way in.

Good and effective accounting software systems have measures in place to counter these risks, like not needing manual data entries and having proper backup of your data to protect your business from any mishaps. It is important to look for software that poses minimum level of risk to your business during and after its implementation.

Chapter 4: Comparing prices

The next most crucial step when selecting accounting software is comparing the prices of different systems. This often turns out to be the most complicated thing to do. The pricing structure is quite complex as there are different types of costs that need to be evaluated carefully before you can figure out your actual investment in the system.

Here are some of the costs that vendors should accurately provide in their quotations:

Total cost of ownership

Most managers make the mistake of selecting accounting software based on the one-time cost they incur when buying the software, or the annual subscription fee quoted by the vendor. However, this is not your total cost of ownership as there are several other future costs that are added to the upfront cost. These include the vendor's license fee, system maintenance fee, annual support and service fee, installation and data transfer fee, hardware costs and training costs.

So, before you pick software for your organization, it is important to calculate the total cost of ownership so that you know the exact amount you are paying for the software. The costs that should be evaluated differ on whether you are buying an on-premises software solution or a Software as a Service (SaaS) solution for your business.

On-premises software typically means you are fully responsible for the installation and ongoing software and hardware maintenance. SaaS solutions usually take all this responsibility from you, but generally can be more costly long term.

Common fees and expenses for "On-Premises" systems

If you are buying on-premises software, it means the ownership of the software would be completely transferred to you. These are the costs you need to consider:

- **Software License –**This is a one-time upfront fee you have to pay for buying the ownership rights to the software. This fee is often charged based on the type of software you have selected and the number of users allowed on the system.

- **Installation -** If your company doesn't have an in-house IT staff, you might have to ask the vendor to install the software at first, for which they would charge an additional fee in most cases. This is an important fee to be paid if you want the system up and running properly.

- **Annual Support and Maintenance** - This fee is optional in most cases and is typically charged once per year based on a particular rate applied to the licensing fee. Paying this fee entitles you to ongoing maintenance services, customer support and access to system upgrades made in future.

- **Customization and Software Configuration** - This is the extra cost you'll have to bear to get the software modified to fit your business needs. This can be a difficult task to achieve so the cost customization is generally a bit high.

- **Data Migration** - Once you have the new software system installed, you will be required to input all previous business data into the system. If you were previously using another system, you will have to transfer the data between the two systems. Again, this is another difficult and time-consuming task so if your vendor is handling it, they might charge extra for it.

- **Staff Training** - All vendors offer to provide basic training to your staff regarding the use of the new software, which is usually free and web-based. However, if you need more comprehensive on-site training from the vendors, you might have to pay extra for it

- **Personal Computer, Server and Other Hardware** - Installing new software always means that you will have to make some hardware upgrades as well, probably adding a new server, getting some powerful computers and having backup devices. For some software, you will have to make more hardware changes than for others so the cost of these upgrades is also included in the cost of the software's total cost of ownership.

- ➤ **Ancillary Service Fees -** If the software needs some ancillary services to operate, they are often charged for separately by the vendors.

Common fees and expenses for (SaaS)

If you are getting Software as a Service, the cost components you have to consider include:

- ➤ **Subscription -** SaaS systems are most commonly made available on a subscription basis compared to the upfront cost you have to pay for buying a software license. Subscription costs can be charged on a monthly, bi-annual or annual basis. While subscription cost is lower than the licensing cost initially, it can accumulate to a larger sum over the years.

- ➤ **Set-Up -** While you won't be required to install the system on your personal computers in the case of an SaaS system, there would still be some minor set-up costs you have to bear such as the fee for configuration of new accounts.

- ➤ **Computer Hardware -** Every program has its own hardware requirements. While most SaaS systems can work on all PCs, there are some that have specific hardware requirements. If your selected software is one of them, the cost of necessary hardware upgrades would also be a part of the total ownership cost.

- **Ancillary Services** - Again, if your software needs the support of some ancillary services to function, they might be priced separately.

- **Training** - Most SaaS vendors offer fee basic web-based training for your employees to help them learn how to use the system. If you need more comprehensive phone-based or on-site training, it might cost you extra.

- **Data Migration** - Whether you had manual records previously or you were using some other system, data will need to be migrated to the new system, which can be a tedious task and the vendors might charge separately for it.

- **Customization and Software Configuration** - While it's not common, SaaS systems can also be customized if you need them to fit your own business needs more closely. For any such customization, you would be required to pay your system vendor an additional sum.

Comparing the quotes

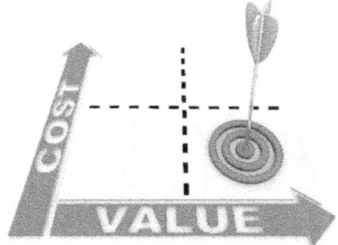

When it comes to comparing the total cost of ownership of software, there are two things to consider: the total upfront cost you have to pay right away and the net present value of all the future costs you will incur. The upfront, non-recurring costs you should add up include software license, customization, installation, data migration, training and hardware. Next, you need to add up the recurring costs which usually include subscription and maintenance fees, and find their Net Present Value.

Then, you need to add the total of both the recurring (NPV) and non-recurring costs, which will give you the total cost of ownership. This is the actual price you have to consider when calculating your return on investment (ROI). You shouldn't always go for the least expensive software.

You should instead pick the one that can be most productive for your company, resulting in the optimal ROI ratio.

Chapter 5: Assess the software vendor's viability

The next tricky part when it comes to selecting the right software is assessing your vendor's viability. Here is a scenario to consider: you get your software, implement it after tedious efforts, train your staff and continue using the system for a few months successfully when suddenly your software vendor goes out of business.

For those who have an SaaS solution, this is one of the worst scenarios as it could put their business in danger. On the other hand, those who own the software would also bear losses as they paid for upgrades, maintenance and a number of other services when buying the software. So, before you make a decision about which accounting software to select, you need to carefully assess the vendor's capability. Here are some financial and strategic factors to consider when assessing your vendor:

- **Balance Sheet** - The balance sheet is the best way to determine a company's financial strength. It shows you whether the company has enough working capital to stay afloat over a long-term period in the future. For this, you should take a look at not just the current financial situation of the company but also its long-term debts.

- **Profitability** - If the vendor is making less than a 10% profit, it leaves them with an extremely narrow cushion to work with, especially in case of emergencies. Moreover, lower profits also indicate that the vendor is less likely to make investments in further development and support.

- **Revenue Size** - A vendor who has more annual revenue is generally considered to be more viable, but this isn't always the best indicator to go with. It all depends on what their expenses are in turn, and how they handle their profit and investments.

- **Ongoing Investment** - It is important to select a vendor who shows his commitment to further product development. Make sure your vendor invests in support and product enhancement and has a proper product roadmap in place.

- **Product Importance to Vendor** - Vendors who are offering more than one product sometimes pay more attention to one product than another, and this isn't a fact their balance sheet would reflect. Assess how important your product category is to the vendor and how much they invest in this category. Often, it's best to go for a vendor who is focused on a single product category or industry.

> **Product Features -** Is the software solution you are getting innovative and differentiated enough to capture investments even if the company is in trouble? If the company needs additional investment, or if it is taken over by another company, the only products that will survive are those that are different from the market. If there are several other solutions like that on the market, it isn't likely to get any support through further investments.

Do your homework properly and don't select a vendor just because their accounting software seems the best at present. Also, don't just rely on the financial viability of the vendors, also consider strategic factors. When you are sure the vendor you have selected isn't at a risk of neglecting the product you are getting or running out of business any time soon, you can select their accounting software.

What about the reseller or Business Partner?

Very few companies have internal resources or the expertise to implement new software applications and will generally choose to work with a Business Partner (BP) or Value-Added Reseller (VAR) for implementation and support. The Distributor or Vendor will typically distribute their products through the BP/Reseller.

It is vital that you find a Business Partner/Reseller who understands your business and user needs. You need to ensure that the consultant has adequate experience both implementing and supporting the solution you choose and can provide references to back up their claims. This consultant will be an important partner in helping you to select, purchase and install your application. It is important that you are comfortable with their style of conducting business, as they will also be maintaining your system.

You also play a vital part in representing your suggestions, this means that your specific requests for items in the application that you would like enhanced or developed are realised through charting them with your Business Partner/reseller.

Before you select a consultant, determine who will be doing the actual implementation once the initial sales process is over—or is the re-seller only interested in closing a sale and moving on?

What about International Financial Reporting Standards (IFRS)?

Accounting products like Sage Evolution adhere to and apply global financial requirements as set out by IFRS (International Financial Reporting Standards). These are principles-based standards, interpretations and the framework (1989) adopted by the International Accounting Standards Board (IASB). Many of the standards forming part of IFRS are known by the older name of International Accounting Standards (IAS). Prior to that we applied GAAP (Generally Accepted Accounting Principles) to refer to the standard framework of guidelines for financial accounting used in any given jurisdiction; generally known as accounting standards. GAAP includes the standards, conventions, and rules accountants follow in recording and summarizing, and in the preparation of financial statements.

Holding to these standards is important because you know that your software is going to adhere to principles that ensure financial accuracy in your business. When systems are not applying these measures it can result in inaccuracies and fraud can occur where editing and regeneration of invoices are possible.

Chapter 6: Implementing the New Accounting Software

Once you have selected the new accounting software that best fits your company's needs, the next step is proper implementation of the software. If you think that's an easy task to complete, you will be surprised when you learn how many things you need to be careful about in order to carry out the implementation successfully.

The best implementation strategy

In order to effectively implement your new accounting software, you need to have a strategy in hand. To give you a nudge in the right direction, here are the steps you should follow to get the most from your software.

```
1. Implementation  →  2. Task Sign-Offs  →  3. Module Go Live
   Planning                                    Approvals
```

1. **Implementation Planning** – After discussing how the software will be implemented with the software vendor, you should consider drafting a plan for implementation. This means that you should schedule the implementation activities and determine the responsibilities of your staff and the delegation of clients' resources.

2. **Implementation Tasks/Sign-Offs** – The documents and procedures to be used in this point will set the foundations for managing risks and ensuring that you take responsibility for the system. In addition, with the help of a checklist, tasks will be performed according to the resources allocated to them and the required timing. However, to minimize the risks that arise during implementation, managing the work through project meetings, on-site management, and internal management will be necessary.

3. **Module Go Live Approvals** – In this process, you will be asked to sign a Go-Live Approval document in order to indicate that you have taken responsibility for that system and are planning to participate actively in the project. Also during this phase, you will need to check for incomplete data conversions. This is when tasks are not being executed the way you want them to. Therefore, consider phased go-lives, which allow you to slowly and gradually integrate the system. This option may be best if your

business is new or if you already have a system in place.

Tips for successful accounting software implementation

The entire implementation process can be comprised of several steps including installation, setup, customization, data migration, user training and gaining expertise in software use. From start to end, this can get extremely complicated and there is a genuine risk something will go wrong, leaving your entire investment at risk. To avoid that and to make this implementation simple, here's what you need to do:

> ➤ **Being realistic** is the first thing you should do, which means making peace with the fact that your business operation might be disturbed for a period of time between days and weeks. Work out an implementation timetable with your software vendor so that you have a clear idea of how long it's going to take for your software to be up and running.

- Whatever accounting system you previously had in place, whether computerized or manual, **clean it up ahead of time**, tying up as many loose ends as possible. This will make the data migration to the new accounting system much more convenient and fast.

- Before you start with the software installation, **make a checklist** of all the necessary hardware changes that need to be made, and make them at once so that you don't have any trouble once the software is installed. Don't make the mistake of underestimating the time each task will take or you will end up with a dysfunctional and invalid timetable. Again, be realistic.

- To keep better track of the implementation process, **break it into several small, manageable phases**. The end of each phase can work as a milestone where you can stop and track how the implementation has worked out so far.

- If your employees need training to use the new system, **don't wait until after the system is implemented to train them**. Instead, start training them beforehand so that, by the time the system is in place, they can start using the software right away, partially if not completely, while they get more hands-on training.

- If you need outside help with any step of the implementation process because your **organization lacks expertise, don't hesitate to get it.** Your vendor can help you with most things and, if not, you can look for other trained professionals.

➢ Also, keep in mind that there are **bound to be some glitches in the system** so keep a margin for these problems in your timetable.

Software implementation game plan checklist

During the implementation process, there are several important tasks you should remember to do. Here is a checklist outlining some of these important tasks:

- ✓ Setting a date for the purchase of the accounting software.
- ✓ Creating a different team to handle every step of the implementation process and assigning them responsibilities clearly.

- ✓ Creating an implementation timeline.
- ✓ Reviewing all necessary software and hardware requirements you need for the software to run smoothly before you start with the installation.

- ✓ Cleaning up your old system and having the previous data streamlined for migration to the new system.

- ✓ Assessing your current processes and finding out how you can improve them to increase productivity.

- ✓ Starting system installation and training of employees, specifically administrators.
- ✓ Creating system customization where needed and testing them.
- ✓ Starting hands-on training, focusing on the end-users of the system.

- ✓ Getting assistance and support from vendors or helpers for the first week or so who can help end-users use the system.

- ✓ Starting data migration to the new accounting software.
- ✓ Getting the system up and running.

Going beyond the Accounting Software Implementation

Don't think that once the accounting software is successfully implemented your work is done. There are a lot of follow-up procedures you need to complete in order to ensure that you took the right decision, the decision works out for your company in the long run and whether further software changes will be needed in the future to increase productivity. Let's take a look at some things you need to look out for:

Reporting, dashboards and alerts

Getting the best out of any system typically comes from the final reporting systems. It's natural to try to control the expense of an implementation, but be careful about cutting this important area. Without meaningful and easy to understand reports your entire investment could be wasted.

Training employees

Since this may be their first time dealing with this type of software, your employees should be well-trained to handle it. To train your employees, you can always bring in a specialized team of trainers with ample knowledge of this software and have them conduct hands-on training sessions at your workplace. This is more convenient than shipping your workers off-site since they will become familiar with the software from their own desks. However, in addition to these sessions, you should consider building reports and booklets to ensure that they have what they learned in writing in case they ever forget what they were taught.

In addition, start with the basics then gradually move on to the complex features of the software. While you may want to teach everything to your employees within a few days, you need to be patient or else they may make errors that affect the system and ultimately your business operations. So, plan when you want your training sessions while the software is in the development stage so that you can avoid major losses while your employees are learning about your new accounting system.

Training aside, you need to ensure that your system receives regular support and maintenance. You should usually discuss this prior to buying the software, but make sure that the vendor keeps their promises later. If you forget this little detail, your accounting software may not serve you as long as you expect and you may eventually have to repeat the whole process after a year or so. So spare yourself the hassle and plan a maintenance schedule to ensure that your system functions perfectly for a long time.

Training for new employees

As new employees are hired, they will require training. Speak with your consultant, and create a training program that is put into place automatically once a new employee comes on board.

Regular system analysis

As time goes by, all systems tend to lose some of their initial levels of efficiency, and all users tend not to report this until the system's efficiency has been significantly impacted.

Rather than waiting for this to happen, establish a system of preventive maintenance, where you and your consultant review the system to see how people are using it. This could be on a monthly basis or on whatever schedule seems to be appropriate. These visits might be more frequent after the system has been installed initially, and then further apart as time passes.

The annual business check-up

While your consultant might visit you on a regular basis, it's a good idea to consider establishing a formal annual review of the system (hardware, software and people).

We recommend a formal analysis of the entire system to assess its overall performance. You might even think of it in the same light as the Preliminary Needs Analysis.

You want to speak to the people using the system to determine their level of satisfaction, and whether they need additional training or additional enhancements, etc. By adopting a formal review process, you and your consultant can take steps to make sure the whole system is operating at optimum efficiency.

Depending on the size of the company and the number of users and applications installed, this review could be accomplished in as little as a few hours, or continue over several days.

GET YOUR BOOK BONUS TODAY:

To get access to our special 55 Page "Software Selection and Implementation Checklist"

Visit www.jefflewis.com.au and email us your receipt as per instructions on the website.

Or Scan this QR Code:

Chapter 7: Summary

For every business, expansion is an inevitable process. With expansion, it is important that you bring necessary changes to your organizational processes and one of these changes is the introduction of sophisticated accounting software in the organization when you need to get things organized. However, selecting the right software isn't always the easiest thing to do. The decision is extremely complicated, and a number of factors have to be evaluated before you decide which software solution is best for you.

Carefully implemented, the right accounting software can be extremely beneficial to your organization. It can make your functions more streamlined and productive, ensuring that your profitability is increased in the long run. From budgeting to tax reporting, selecting good accounting software can solve a lot of problems for your organization in a seamless manner.

Chapter 8: Next Steps

In this book we have covered all aspects of deciding on the right accounting software for your business and how to go about the various stages including implementation. The next step is to actually go to the marketplace and start your assessment on the best solution for you.

The reason we wrote this book was to educate business people on the best way to find, evaluate, purchase and implement your chosen solution.

At **Usage Business Solutions** we have deep industry experience providing the best of breed accounting and ERP solutions. Below we detail our flagship product, **Sage Evolution**.

Australian businesses have taken hold of Sage Evolution and what business management software can mean to them in their business efficiency. Statistics show that these 175 companies have upgraded their business process with these results:

- ✓ 23% lower operating costs
- ✓ 22% lower administrative costs
- ✓ 28% lower inventory costs
- ✓ 29% improvement in obsolete inventory

Why did they finally make the move? These survey stats show:

- ✓ 53% needed to replace outdated technology
- ✓ 45% recognized cost advantage of Evolution
- ✓ 28% seeking more functionality
- ✓ 20% recognized their business was changing
- ✓ 20% implemented a consolidation strategy in their business (branches, outlets, multiple sites)

What are the Features of Sage Evolution?

Sage Evolution delivers an entire business management solution. Its database guarantees data integrity and keeps all your data in one central database. Our product is proven unique and effective among the rest. This product has exceptional features and here they are:

- **Contact Relationship Management** – It gives you a chance to track, analyze and handle customer and supplier interactions. This allows you to be proactive in sustaining their needs or exceeding their primary demands.

- **Incident Tracking System** – This feature allows you to find everything you want. You can find the summarized information or the detailed transactions to source your documents. You are free to do this within a single click of your mouse.

- **Receivables and Payables** – This gives you instant access to supplier and customer balances. You can also use this to check overdue totals, sales and purchase history.

- **Sales and Purchase Order Entry** – This feature lets you maintain and handle outstanding orders, back orders and processed orders. It also integrates fully into payable, receivable and inventory modules.

- **Inventory Control** – Our accounting software provides you with great control over your business stock. This system offers both detailed operational reports and summary management reports. These reports can be easily customized.
- **Annuity Billing** – This feature integrates with inventory and receivables. It also provides repetitive invoices on a daily, monthly or quarterly basis. It is designed to take care of your company billing function and invoice.
- **Manufacturing** - This software allows you to see a full audit trail of every manufacturing process. It also draws stock at the beginning of the production method and reverses any unused stock once it is completed. This can also help in creating by-products to your main production item.

For the best accounting functions, Sage Evolution also offers several features such as general ledger for Microsoft Office integration, unit of measure for import cost allocations, account consolidations and job costing.

Other essential features include information alerts, multi-currency, business gateway, bank statement manager and a lot more. With the comprehensive range of features in the Sage Evolution software package, our product provides scalable, strong and flexible financial management for your growing business.

What Makes Sage Evolution More Effective than Others?

Sage Evolution offers you the following benefits:

- ✓ Regular Updates
- ✓ Complete Upgrades
- ✓ Exclusive Email Support
- ✓ Handles your finances
- ✓ Improves your relationship with your customers, employees and suppliers
- ✓ First-Line Telephonic Support and a lot more!

Sage Evolution takes your accounting operation to the next level. Its powerful features employ reliable technology that allows greater flexibility in your financials.

We would welcome the opportunity to show you our range of products and provide a totally free and no obligation system review with one of our experienced business partners. Simply go to www.sageevolution.com.au and book today or give us a call and we would be happy to help.

GET YOUR BOOK BONUS TODAY:

To get access to our special 55 Page "Software Selection and Implementation Checklist" Visit www.jefflewis.com.au and email us your receipt as per instructions on the website. Or Scan this QR Code:

The Book You Need Before You Buy That Accounting Software

Chapter 9: Case studies

Company: Rolls Royce

Software used: Sage Pastel Evolution

Rolls-Royce Marine Australia, develops, designs, supplies and supports marine products and systems for naval and commercial customers worldwide. The global business provides integrated power systems for use on land, at sea and in the air.

With a primary focus on power, propulsion and motion control solutions, Rolls-Royce Marine Australia serves over 2,000 customers and has equipment installed on 30,000 vessels operating around the world. Rolls-Royce Marine Australia has four business units, which focus on Merchant, Naval, Offshore and Submarines market segments. A strong focus on research and development has seen Rolls-Royce Marine Australia become the pioneer of many important marine technologies that include; aero derivative marine gas turbines, controllable pitch propellers and waterjets.

"Time is valuable, and to save me two days per month is priceless" – Jamie Kilsby, Financial Controller.

The Challenge

Rolls-Royce Marine Australia's accounting program was struggling to process the day-to-day running of the business. The number of staff that could access the system simultaneously was limited causing the program to slow down and cause data integrity issues. It was becoming a big frustration amongst staff and management. 'Often the system would only post to one side of the trial balance so the figures were not always right and it took a lot of time to fix the problems the software was creating' said Jamie Kilsby, financial controller for Rolls-Royce Marine Australia, WA.

The business was on the lookout for a solution that could manage large amounts of data on products and customers details as well as manage multiple users on the system at the one time. It was time to upgrade!

The Solution

A robust solution that will grow with the business.

Sage Pastel Evolution is a robust solution with an advanced operating environment. The SQL database ensures data integrity and scalability. It also allows the business to tailor the program to meet individual organisational needs. 'We needed something with Tax Management, Job Costing, Fixed Assets, CRM and all the standard accounting modules to run the complex business'.

Business Partner, Progressive Business Technologies presented Rolls-Royce Marine Australia with Sage Pastel Evolution and immediately Jamie found the system easy-to-use. 'The layout of the system tree makes it so easy to jump between the modules. I knew that introducing the system to the staff wouldn't be a problem'.

The ability to raise Purchase Orders and capture costs associated to the job was important.

Being a Job Driven Company it was important that Rolls Royce Marine Australia has the ability to raise purchase orders against a job, as well as capture all other costs and revenue associated with the Job to identify profitability.

The CRM module, which is the core of the program stores email communication within the client contact. Each time a staff member view's a client folder, they are able to see all the communication which has been sent to the client. The central storage area of the program provides valuable historical communication for staff. Staff have all the historical communication they need to maintain and develop a meaningful relationship with the client.

This provides a valuable tool when you have several departments and staff members dealing with the one customer.

The Results

Since implementing Sage Paste Evolution, Rolls Royce Marine Australia has experienced a number of efficiencies in their day-to-day running of the business.

The purchase order template functionality has proven to be an effective time saver, where users have the capability to create a copy of the Order Acknowledgement as a Purchase order without having to recapture the information. The template is also used during the quotation process and has minimised staff errors and streamlined the order process.

Company: Medical Sales and Service

Software used: Sage Pastel Evolution

Medical Sales and Service has grown considerably since opening their doors in 1975. The business was established to fulfil a need in the Western Australian health care market for the servicing of medical equipment in the areas of anaesthetics, resuscitation, respiratory/oxygen therapy and infant care.

As the business continued to grow, they expanded their services to include the sale of medical products which complimented the equipment servicing business.

"We were very happy with Progressive Business Technologies and there on-site assistance during the implementation and transition to Sage Pastel Evolution". Rod Dowding, Sales Manager.

The Challenge

Medical Sales & Service were using an entry level accounting solution which worked well when the business was small. However by 2005, the business had expanded and the existing accounting package was struggling to perform basic daily tasks. The accounting solution was not integrated with the business' CRM solution and the sales team were left with the laborious task of entering the same information into two separate programs. It was crippling the sales team with additional administration duties and taking them away from face-to-face customer interaction.

Rod Dowding, Sales Manager for Medical Sales and Services, manages a team of sales representatives who are on the road visiting clients regularly. Previously, Rod spent countless hours manually segmenting sales figures to record the sales activity for each team member and each product and service. Upon completing the data segmentation, only then was Rod able to have a true understanding of the profitability of each division to then calculate sales team bonuses based on their individual performances.

The Solution

Sage Pastel Evolution's General Ledger was introduced for divisional reporting.

Medical Sales and Services has the ability to capture individual sales figures for two divisions within the one client. 'We have a hospital which uses our Service Division as well as purchases from our Consumable Division, so it's important that we keep the two businesses separate but keep them connected to manage and report on the one business'.

Simple CRM and sales force automation are tightly interwoven into Sage Pastel Evolution.

Sales staff have the ability to enter a lead into the system against a prospect. You can create quotations and simply convert the prospect to a customer and at the same time, the quote to an invoice without having to re-key any of the information. 'My sales team are quite happy to work on the system now, they find it quick and easy to write an order, especially since the lead is in there already'.

Sage Pastel Evolution allows you to capture communication with the customer in one area. The information helps sales staff stay informed and manage business relationships effectively and efficiently. Customizable reporting is simple in Sage Pastel Evolution.

Progressive Business Technologies made further customizations to the data grid views to allow Medical Sales & Service to view data in the way they want to see it. By customizing the grid view, they have the ability to produce reports quickly and simply.

The Results

Rod has the ability to track the sales team's progress on the fly. With deeper insight, Rod can address the changes immediately. "I can download the report at any time and graph the current sales against each team member and immediately establish if there is a problem. Act on it straight away before it leads to an unsatisfied customer or staff member".

The sales team have the ability to manage the progression of leads, orders and invoices out on the road. The process facilitates sales momentum which empowers and motivates the team. 'It's important to keep your staff motivated and have the ability to address a drop in sales'. Sage Pastel Evolution provides me with the tools to see this at anytime from anywhere".

Company: Footprint Books

Software used: Sage Pastel Evolution

Celebrating their 10th year in business, Footprint Books is a total distribution service, incorporating the sales, marketing and warehousing of high quality, Academic and Specialist books.

The business has over 92,000 book titles representing publishers from the USA, UK, Canada & New Zealand with an annual turnover exceeding $6.8 million. The distribution and warehousing facility is based in Sydney employing 20 people.

The business goal is to make educational and reference material available for professionals, business people, students and lovers of learning in the Australasian marketplace

The Challenge

Footprint Books were facing daily challenges, their existing financial package would only allow ten users to simultaneously access the system. This software also lacked features inhibiting the advanced processing needs of their growing business.

The challenge is to find a solution that can incorporate the financial aspects of the business with detailed inventory and order management. The solution must have the capacity to store over 92,000 book titles each containing large amounts of indexed and searchable information. The stored information is used by customers to easily search for book titles when purchasing online.

The Solution

Sage Pastel Evolution was implemented along with additional modules from Systems Practice 'SP Toolkit' which assisted with the automation of the business processes and the development of electronic communication to customers.

Automated ordering and dispatch a breeze with Sage Pastel Evolution

Orders are received by phone, fax and the website. Upon receipt the orders are allocated through the Order Allocation module which assigns existing stock to the orders based on various criteria such as urgent orders and oldest order date. Once the allocation is complete, the module prints picking slips for all orders with allocated stock. Orders then move on to the Scan Pack Module which allows the warehouse to pick and pack the allocated quantity using barcode scanners. This part of the process ensures that the correct books and quantities are picked for the order.

Systems Practice 'SP Toolkit' integrates with Sage Pastel Evolution

The SP Toolkit comprises a range of add-on modules covering warehousing and inventory management. The modules used by Footprint Books are: Branch Transfer, Scan Pack, Scan Receive, Dispatch, Reorder, Order Allocation, Import Cost and CRM Assist. Each module has been interwoven into the core of Sage Pastel Evolution to create the automated ordering and re-order process.

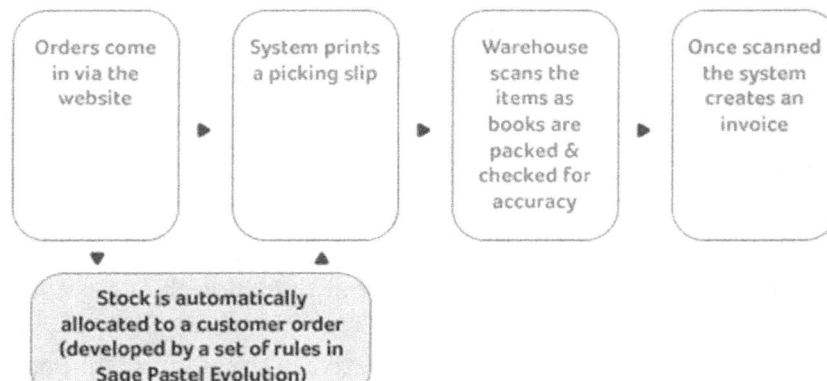

The Results

Sage Pastel Evolution is a robust flexible solution that integrates with additional modules to facilitate the automation of business processes.

Footprint Books has increased staff productivity and reduced staff numbers since implementation. 'Things don't get caught in a blind alley anymore, the system prompts you when something has been missed', said Simon Player, Part Owner and Director of Footprint Books.

Sage Pastel Evolution's SQL database is a robust foundation which can manage extensive indexed and searchable information for 92,000+ book titles. Footprint Books can rest assured that the solution will continue to grow with the business.

GET YOUR BOOK BONUS TODAY:

To get access to our special 55 Page "Software Selection and Implementation Checklist"

Visit www.jefflewis.com.au and email us your receipt as per instructions on the website.

Or Scan this QR Code:

www.ingramcontent.com/pod-product-compliance
Lightning Source LLC
Chambersburg PA
CBHW071756170526
45167CB00003B/1052